A Metaphor for Life

How life,
personal metamorphosis
and faith intertwine

WTL INTERNATIONAL

A Metaphor for Life

Copyright © 2025 Simone Spellen
WTL International has obtained
publishing rights.

All rights reserved. No part of this publication may be reproduced in any form or by any electronic or mechanical means, including information storage and material systems, except in the case of brief quotations embodied in critical articles or reviews, without permission in writing from its publisher,
WTL International.

Published by
WTL International
930 North Park Drive
P.O. Box 33049
Brampton, Ontario
L6S 6A7 Canada
www.wtlipublishing.com

Publication date: November 28, 2025

ISBN 978-1-77831-076-8

DEDICATION

To the glory of God
and in loving memory of
my mother who taught me to pray

In loving memory of
my courageous Aunt Edda;
an insatiably inquisitive mind who,
throughout her life,
exemplified how to embrace
living outside of comfort and
knowledge

TABLE OF CONTENTS

Foreword ...1

Introduction ...3

Chapter 1 A Butterfly Danced ...9

Chapter 2 Awakened in My Soul ...17

Chapter 3 Conflicts and Conflagrations ...25

Chapter 4 Born Again ...33

Epilogue ...43

FOREWORD

Meeting Edda the first time, I felt an immediate bond with her. Since then, our relationship has grown to sisterhood where we appreciate each other. She is humble and yet strongly opiniated. She is definitively a researcher, and through this topic, shows us what an important part of her belief this has been and of her continuous growth.

This all makes sense to me, and Edda captures well the beautiful growth of the human being through comparison to the butterfly. Two keywords here, "Metaphor" and "Change."

Easy to read, with a lot of room for reflection in between the pages, A *Metaphor for Life* makes you stop, pause, and wonder at the amazing God we serve.

~Nancy C. Marecki Stevenson

INTRODUCTION

A Metaphor for Life was conceived out of a desire to tell my story of being born again in Jesus Christ and finding joy, peace, and contentment in my walk with Him.

I was born in an Anglican church community, baptized as an infant, and confirmed at twelve years of age. I grew up in the church, teaching Sunday School, signing in the choir, and serving in any other capacity I was asked to serve.

After immigrating to Canada, I was exposed to various other denominations of Christianity and also numerous religions. As a teacher, I came into contact with students of various faiths and I began a long search to find understanding of these different perceptions of God, the meaning of this plurality of worship and where and how I fit into the scheme of things.

I found the Baha'i Faith and thought I had arrived at my final destination. I followed this way for over thirty years, but there was something missing. I could not put my finger on it, but there was a hunger in my soul for a purpose and meaning to my life.

One of the fundamental teachings of the Baha'i Faith is that the purpose of life is to know God and to worship Him. Yet, they teach that we cannot know God except through His manifestations who are the prophets of all religions. Every one of the prophets taught a different perception of God.

When my parents died, the hunger in my soul intensified and I sought ways of relieving my grief and sorrow. I turned to the Bible and found in the Psalms solace for my anguish. My journal, in those days, had consisted of cries for help, desperate cries to the God who created me and was supposed to see all my troubles.

One night, at about two o'clock in the morning, I turned on the television to see if there was anything there that could bring relief from the loneliness I felt. There was a preacher appealing to all who were watching to turn to Jesus for help and deliverance from whatever

INTRODUCTION

problems they were experiencing at the time. His words seemed tailored to my situation, and I felt that he was speaking directly to me. "Come unto me, all ye that labour and are heavy laden, and I will give you rest," he said, quoting Jesus in the Scriptures (Matthew 11:28). "For God so loved the world, that he gave his only begotten Son, that whosoever believeth in him should not perish, but have everlasting life," he continued (John 3:16). He later invited all who were watching to repeat after him a prayer that would signify our acceptance of Jesus, repentance from sin and a willingness to be led by Him. I repeated the prayer and along with my acceptance of Jesus Christ as my Lord and Saviour, I requested the offer of a publication called *Now What?* which was free for the taking. This simple step was the beginning of a profound change in my psyche.

As I studied the gospel of John, which came to me in the mail a few days later, the troubles of my heart and soul began to melt away. Joy, peace, and contentment, together with whispers of love, replaced the confusion and loss which I had been experiencing. I was born again.

A METAPHOR FOR LIFE

Butterflies (*real* butterflies) seemed to follow me wherever I went, as if confirming my newness of life. They seemed to bear on their delicate wings a message of victory and a freedom of spirit. At the Niagara Parks Butterfly Conservatory in Niagara Falls, Ontario, I found out that the Greek word for butterfly is "psyche." I began to research the butterfly and found in one book, on the page with a picture of the cocoon, a copy of a painting of Mary and Joseph fleeing with the Christ Child to Egypt.

I made a connection between the spirit that made the butterfly and the spirit of Christ. I made a connection between the journey of becoming a butterfly and Jesus' journey. Jesus' earthly life was to end in an agonizing death on the cross and to be regained in the victory and triumph of His resurrection. At His resurrection, Jesus was glorified. He received a glorified body. Being born again is a type of metamorphosis. One who is born again receives a new heart and a new life.

In 2 Corinthians 5:17, Paul writes, "Therefore if any man be in Christ, he is a new creature; old things are passed away; behold all things are become

INTRODUCTION

new." The butterfly symbolizes this newness of life. *A Metaphor for Life* is an attempt to give meaning to the experiences of life; the twists and turns, the pain and suffering, the darkness before the light, the change that only God can make and the uniqueness of Jesus Christ, His Son, among all the prophets.

A METAPHOR FOR LIFE

1

A BUTTERFLY DANCED

It was a long, harsh drought. No longer the verdant, flourishing pastures inhabited by various life forms, fields were now abandoned. Desperate farmers had fled in search of food for their surviving herds. Under the fierce and fiery blast of the sun, the soil had hardened and cracked into squares with massive holes like pores in the ground.

The dry, parched earth cried out for rain and when the rain came it was a thunderous downpour beating upon the ground as if summoning life again. The thirsty earth responded and, inch by inch, it closed its gaping pores.

A METAPHOR FOR LIFE

Soon, a fresh, moist bed of comfort arrived. Seeds lying dormant above and below the ground, burst their coats and yielded up the new life within. Blades of grass along with thorns, thistles, and tender flowers began to form a new world of colour: red, green, blue, yellow, and purple. A diversity of moving life forms gradually returned to cohabit the fields. They buzzed, hummed, hissed and chirped their hymns of praise and thanksgiving for a new day and a fresh start.

Out of eternity, before time, came the

Word that became a butterfly.

In the midst of it all, a butterfly danced. Light and magical, it flitted from flower to flower. Small, delicate, and free, its movement through the air was a picture of grace, and beauty. It was a sight for reflection.

From a dark encasement all shrouded in mystery, this butterfly had emerged. Its colourful dance was both a story and a song. The theme was transformation. The story is old, yet ever new. The song is an expression of hope, rebirth, and regeneration. Here is a metaphor for the cyclical nature of life and the inevitability of change. Here too is a symbol of the beginning in the end, a new beginning.

In the beginning was the void, the potential for the vast universe, a universe pregnant with all life. 'In the beginning, God created the heaven and the earth, and the earth was without form, and void, and darkness was upon the face of the deep. And the Spirit of God moved upon the face of the water. And God said, let there be light and there was light' (Genesis 1:1–3). Thus, was the manner in which all the heavens and the earth were finished, and all the host of them. Out of eternity, before time, came the Word that became a butterfly.

Through time, we have the privilege of witnessing elements of creation such as butterflies go through stages of development. We become aware that a human being grows from a tiny embryo, through the foetal stage, into an infant. An infant grows through stages into adulthood. We can relate this process to that of a seed as it germinates into a new plant, producing hundreds of seeds.

A METAPHOR FOR LIFE

Many years ago, as a young schoolgirl in one of the primary grades, I learned a poem about the beginning, and the growth of a plant from a seed. It follows here, under the title of "The Little Plant."

The Little Plant

In the heart of a seed,
Buried deep, so deep,
A dear little plant
Lay fast asleep.

"Wake!" said the sunshine,
"And creep to the light."
"Wake!" said the voice
Of the raindrops bright.

The little plant heard
And it rose to see
What a wonderful outside world
might be.

~Kate Louise Brown

A BUTTERFLY DANCED

As part of our appreciation of the poem, each student was given two lima beans. The first seed was opened to reveal the baby plant "asleep" inside. The other seed was placed in a glass jar lined with a water-soaked sheet of blotting paper, and made to rest between the jar and the paper. The paper was constantly being moistened to avoid it drying out. Exposed to light, warmth, and air, the little plant seemed to grow right before our eyes. We watched the roots grow down, and the leaves rise up above the rim of the jar on their slender stems, as if guided by unseen hands.

Morning could not come soon enough for my classmates and me. We raced to school each day, long before the bell, driven to the windowsill by the prospect of witnessing what was, to us, nothing short of a miracle. What a profound experience was in store for us as we came to realize that in order for the new plant to grow, the "mother" bean had to give up her life. As the young bean plant grew bigger, the parent bean became smaller until it eventually disappeared, adsorbed as food for the new life.

A METAPHOR FOR LIFE

Takeaway(s)

A BUTTERFLY DANCED

Takeaway(s)

2

AWAKENED IN MY SOUL

Whether or not she was aware of it, our teacher, who by now in our eyes was the greatest in the school, had awakened in my soul the seed of appreciation for the spiritual reality of all things. The spirit of awe and wonder generated by the seed exercise has never left me, and the perception of this phenomenon as one of the great themes of life has grown with each participation in and observation of the affairs of our world. I never looked at a seed again without thinking of the potential within, the new life just waiting to burst out.

The spirit of sacrifice and of willingness to surrender to the highest good, seems to be one of the eternal principles. Just as a seed must die for new seeds to be born, a butterfly eventually dies, but not before laying an abundance of eggs, potential for new butterflies.

We can view the development of the butterfly and the process it undergoes in its transition from an egg to adult as a metaphor for life on several levels. On one level, it is symbolic of the changing fortunes of our individual lives. On another level, it is symbolic of challenges facing interrelationships on this earth, the planet we call home with all the forces impacting it since the dawn of time.

Individually and collectively, we are the story of the butterfly and, individually and collectively, we sing our own song as we dance the dance of life. The content, the style, the language, the rhythm, and so forth vary, but the underlying themes and preoccupations bear striking similarities. For example, there are many species of butterflies, but they are all butterflies. We, human beings, come with assorted colours, shapes, sizes, and dispositions, but we are all human beings. Our needs are quite similar. We all want to feel secure, to love and be loved, to be respected and to have our daily needs for food, shelter and protection met. We all change, and we are all aware of forces impacting our individual and collective lives, some forces, within our control, and some, not. For instance, we generally choose our friends, where we live, the food we eat. However, none of us chose to be born in a particular race, place, time or circumstance, neither our capacities for different functions. All of us will experience some kind of change in our lives and, as we change, we effect change.

As it changes from a tiny egg to an adult creature, a butterfly undergoes phases of growth. When the growing stages are over, all that remains is for the chrysalis to crack open the cocoon and for the butterfly to emerge. Within the unmoving chrysalis, such tremendous change has taken place that when this happens, a new creature is born.

Visible, both in the natural world and in the lives of human beings, are the processes of change: of life and death, birth and rebirth, breaking down to build anew. In short, there is a constant renewal and affirmation of life as we endeavour to move forward in time towards a destiny that is often unclear.

The impact of change is evident amply throughout life. The recent increase in changing technologies has enabled us to know one another as individuals and as whole societies. We feel and recognize the consequences of change. Change is inevitable. Every change or unwillingness to change in one part of the world has a ripple effect on the others.

Visible, both in the natural world

and in the lives of human beings,

are the processes of change:

of life and death, birth, and rebirth,

breaking down to build anew.

It is worth noting that in many instances of change, the expressed desire is for something better. Accordingly, in the case of the butterfly, it would appear that there is an invisible, mysterious force propelling us in a direction of change, and change for the better. When a life is touched by this force, such tremendous change takes place that a new, more striking, creature is born.

Through true change, everyday routines that once satisfied our existence no longer seem adequate. As pain and suffering on the physical level has its parallels on the more subtle emotional and psychological levels, emotional and psychological confusion can be daunting. Nevertheless, finding purpose and meaning in life is chaotic and confusing. Changing the status quo to get to a place where we can find our purpose and meaning, and changing to become a version of ourselves that can fulfil this purpose and meaning, are probably the greatest challenges facing us as individuals and as the world community we have become. The importance of change, the glory in change, and the struggle of change cannot be understated, and this epitome of change—the butterfly—greatly exemplifies the process.

A METAPHOR FOR LIFE

Takeaway(s)

_____

_____

_____

_____

_____

_____

_____

_____

_____

_____

_____

_____

_____

_____

_____

_____

_____

_____

AWAKENED IN MY SOUL

Takeaway(s)

3

CONFLICTS AND CONFLAGRATIONS

Conflicts and conflagrations of war bombard our sensibilities daily. Very few people feel secure and many scurry back and forth in search of peace, comfort, and security. Extremes of wealth and poverty dictate our individual worth. Yet rich and poor alike will undergo stages of growth and development that transform us. Like the butterfly, we must travel the road that refines and redefines our character and our divine soul.

Our character, our strife and propensity for differences and conflict, our pettiness and other immaturities, our morals, and eventually, our whole existence, this entire world, must change to constitute a higher, purer state. This is another phase of change the butterfly's life cycle perfectly characterizes.

Made in the image and likeness of God, we have the potential to be beautiful and good, to bring light and hope to others. The restitution and full potential of humankind is promised at the end of time, a euphoric spiritual state depicted in the book of Revelation in the Bible.

> "And I heard a great voice out of heaven saying, Behold, the tabernacle of God is with men, and he will dwell with them, and they shall be his people, and God himself shall be with them, and be their God. And God shall wipe away all tears from their eyes; and there shall be no more death, neither sorrow, nor crying, neither shall there be any more pain: for the former things are passed away" (Revelation 21:3–4 KJV).

The stages of the butterfly provide a ready metaphor for the spiritual implications of the journey that will bring us to this place. From its beginning, from a tiny egg, a caterpillar is born. Like a child, this is the stage of carefree enjoyment of life. Actions are spontaneous, impulse driven. The pleasures of the appetite abound: eating and drinking, making choices, abandoning choices, exploring and testing situations. Life is simple. It is interesting to learn that the caterpillar, before entering the next stage, experiences a "mood change." It becomes nervous, restless, and unsettled. It crawls up a number of trees and hurriedly crawls down, still dissatisfied until it finally settles into some tangle of branches. And all of this after it has shed its skin four times because of eating and growing out of it. We can apply this behaviour to a child growing from infancy through various changes. It is also applicable to the adolescent who feels the impulses and the promptings of adulthood and struggles to find his/her place in the transition. Furthermore, the analogy is mirrored in civilization.

Having emerged from stages of simplicity, civilization has gained complexity and changed eras a few times.

A METAPHOR FOR LIFE

The world now teeters on the edge. It is being propelled towards a greater metamorphosis. It is in an adolescent world struggling to em-brace the reality of this change. It is a spiritual struggle to shed old ways, old beliefs, old customs, and practices which do not support the highest good purposed by our Divine Creator.

Made in the image

and likeness of God, we have

the potential to be beautiful and

good, to bring light and

hope to others.

The apparent agitation of the caterpillar symbolizes the restless hunger that drives us to discover who we are and what we were meant to be. Just as the potential for becoming a butterfly lies within its movement from egg to caterpillar to chrysalis, so the potential for a new and better self, and ultimately, for a new and better world, lies within our willingness to change. It is a change that is summed up in the prayer, "Thy will be done in earth, as it is in heaven" (Matthew 6:10 KJV). It is in the cocoon that the chrysalis is essentially surrendered to the will of heaven. It is here that the individual is born again.

A METAPHOR FOR LIFE

Takeaway(s)

CONFLICTS AND CONFLAGRATIONS

Takeaway(s)

4

BORN AGAIN

We must be born again. Jesus said, "Except a man be born again, he cannot see the kingdom of God" (John 3:3 KJV). It is by way of surrender that hearts are changed, and changed hearts then manifest themselves in changed lives, which in turn eventually produce changed societies. William James in his book *The Varieties of Religious Experience* writes, "The personality is changed, the man is born anew, whether or not his psychological idiosyncrasies are what gave shape to his metamorphosis." Paul, the great apostle of Jesus Christ wrote, "If any man be in Christ, he is a new creature" (2 Corinthians 5:17 KJV).

A METAPHOR FOR LIFE

The creative word "Be" lights the dark world of the cocoon so that the chrysalis becomes a butterfly. Ironically, it seems that for us human beings, in order to experience that light, we must go through the dark worlds of life's difficult events. Nicodemus sought that light as he went to Jesus in the dark of night and, as a result, received understanding from the Master Himself. Saul's dramatic conversion was precipitated through a light that pierced the darkness of his sinful acts and brought about his ultimate surrender to the will of God. Many of us have sought that light as we desire to change. It would seem, then, that if we are to advance into knowledge, wisdom, and understanding, we must experience our own darkness, each according to his/her particular journey, purpose, and destiny. There is joy, and gladness that light up a soul that becomes as a butterfly. It is especially welcome after the period of darkness the cocoon presents. So it will be for those societies that embrace the will and purpose of the Creator.

It is the Creator's will that we love Him and love our neighbours as ourselves. The Master Teacher, Jesus

Christ, shows us the way but there are obstacles that hinder our growth from a caterpillar to a butterfly.

Racism and discrimination are huge stumbling blocks. Fear of the unknown keeps us bogged down in a perpetual state of prejudice, self-centredness and resentment. The unwillingness to be humble in our dealings with one another makes us agitated with mistrust, doubts, destructive thoughts, and feelings of superiority in some, inferiority, and inadequacy in others. Just as human beings come to realize the contributions of each part of the body to the whole, so must there be a recognition by each nation of the contribution of other nations towards a healthy world in all its aspects. I have found this to be a major area needing change. The beauty in the diversity of creation eludes us if we refuse to shed ignorance, and fear of one another.

To arrive at this point of awareness, we, like the caterpillar, must enter our own cocoon. Inside this case, hidden from mortal eyes is a chrysalis: a caterpillar in transition towards becoming a butterfly. The sharpest lens of a camera can never reveal the profound changes taking place. Only God knows what take place here and how. Only His hands accomplish the meticulous, fine-tuning manoeuvres that can bring about the change we see in a newborn butterfly.

The chrysalis stage symbolizes the deepest, most profound changes that occur with the human soul on the journey towards the purpose and destiny the Creator has willed for it. It represents the past and the present, moving towards the ultimate achievement: that which we were meant to be. At the societal level, the past must inform the present and set the nation on a path towards a more beautiful and pleasing world. Like gold that must be fired to bring out the finest quality, it is here in the cocoon that, as individuals, and societies we face, embrace, and overcome all that is uncomfortable and self-serving in order to be transformed into new and better persons serving others in a new and better world.

Newness of life and the joy of the new birth often come after a period of great suffering. It has been shown, time, and time again, that the best spiritual qualities, those that influence the world for good are usually born out of great suffering. Walking "through the valley of the shadow of death" (Psalm 23:4 KJV), we experience "the dark night of the soul" (coined by St. John of the Cross). At the highest mystical level, it is Jesus' flight into Egypt, Jesus' forty days and forty nights in the wilderness, the Garden of Gethsemane, the Cross, and the Sepulchre.

The chrysalis stage symbolizes the deepest, most profound changes that occur with the human soul on the journey towards the purpose and destiny the Creator has willed for it.

Although the suffering is almost unbearable, the victory at the end is never won for the self alone but for all who are willing to benefit from the outcome. It is here that we come to know who we are and what we were meant to be. It is the place of becoming for the average person, but it is here also that the prophet, the seer, the visionary, and the mystic are born. The pressures of life exert a spiritual affection and a new person, a new society, a new world is born.

To be inspired by the butterfly to the fullest is to see its process of change as analogous to the journey of the human soul, and the triumph of the spirit. Taking a lesson from the butterfly, human beings, the highest form of life on Earth, may witness, with the eye of the spirit the working of that mysterious power of an invisible God whose will is always towards the highest good.

"And God saw every thing that he had made, and, behold, it was very good" (Genesis 1:31 KJV). Through the loss of Eden, a long and harsh drought has settled on the souls of humankind. The thirsty and cracked ground has cried out. The rains came through our Lord Jesus Christ. He is "the Way, the Truth and the Life" (John 14:6). By accepting Him, we have access to the All-Loving Creator who is ready and willing to recreate us and bring us to the joy and beauty of the new earth, a new Eden. This is the life eternal.

Each of us is a butterfly in the making. Our cocoons may hang in different places and at different times, but we are all seeds of eternity planted in time. When we acknowledge this, we realize great empathy towards our fellow human beings. Our song and dance express this empathy.

That Is Why I Understand

You have your troubles,
And I have mine,
And that is why I understand.

You have your pain,
And I have mine,
And that is why I understand.

Crying out in dark despair,
You wonder if anyone is out there.
I hear.
I want you to know
That I have been there,
And that is why I understand.

A METAPHOR FOR LIFE

Takeaway(s)

BORN AGAIN

Takeaway(s)

EPILOGUE

True and lasting change can only be executed by God through Jesus Christ. Just as He makes a butterfly from a caterpillar, He can make of anyone a beautiful creature full of love, peace, joy, and compassion. What He does for one on a personal and individual level, He can do collectively for any country or society if leaders turn to Him, seek His truth, and obey His commandments.

Drought will give way to abundant rain, and the new birth will be "a well of water springing up into everlasting life" (Jesus in John 4:14 KJV). Faith and hope are awakened, redefined, and strengthened. Love is no longer a concept cliched into abstraction but is realized in the highest demonstrable concrete acts that embody respect, caring, compassion and empathy. Courage takes the place of fear. Dismissing fear results in a feeling of inner peace and contentment. Contentment with the highest will and purpose, that of the Creator, releases new energy, and ultimately, a new life: a regenerated organism.

Everyone is a butterfly in the making. Our cocoons may hang in different places and at different times, but we are all seeds of eternity planted in time to reflect the power, the beauty and the majesty of God, and His infinite love of diversity. The common thread in the diversity of our humanity with all its implications for physique, emotion, intellect, and spirit is the spark of the Divine.

About the Author

Edda Morgan-Piva was born in Jamaica and migrated to Canada in 1967. She taught in several Toronto schools and eventually settled in Niagara Falls, Ontario with her husband Bruno Piva. She was a member of the Seventh-day Adventist Church Community.

Image Credits:

Abstract background by kvitkanastroyu at 123RF.com, front cover

Common Tiger Butterfly image by prinprince at 123RF.com, front cover

www.ingramcontent.com/pod-product-compliance
Lightning Source LLC
Chambersburg PA
CBHW071917070526
44583CB00016B/2023